HOW TO DEAL WITH A

NARCISSITIC MOTHER IN LAW

11 Personal and Potent

Strategies for Building Harmony

in Your Marriage and Family

Copyright © 2023 by Viola Jacob

KINDLY SCAN THIS CODE TO SEE OTHER BOOKS BY THIS AUTHOR AND REACH OUT TO ME FOR ANY ENQUIRIES VIA CONSULTWITHVIOLA@GMAIL.COM

TABLE OF CONTENT

INTRODUCTION: SHARING MY JOURNEY

In matrimony, unforeseen challenges often present themselves, demanding resilience and wisdom to weave through the dynamics of family systems. Welcome to my story, where I'll share the ups and downs of dealing with a difficult mother-in-law. This book is all about helping you not just survive but thrive despite the challenges. This book, born from my own transformative journey, aims to shed light on how to navigate a relationship with a narcissistic mother-in-law. As I invite you into my world, sharing the triumphs and tribulations, the pages ahead will unfold a guide to not only survive but thrive in the face of such complexities.

I faced a tough situation with my mother-in-law that shook up my happy marriage. The early years were rough, filled with emotional struggles and tricky mind games. But I didn't give up. Instead, I decided to figure out how to make things better. The chapters ahead will reveal how I turned frustration into strength, sharing the steps I took to build a better relationship with my mother-in-law.

To make this journey work, it's important to understand what makes a mother-in-law act the way she does. The key traits of a narcissistic mother-in-law are that she craves attention, lacks understanding, and uses tricky ways to get what she wants. Understanding this behavior is like unlocking a code, helping you deal with the confusion and frustration. Through simple stories and a look into the psychology behind it all, we'll uncover why mothers-in-law act the way they do. This knowledge is the foundation for the practical strategies that follow, helping you handle the challenges and make your marriage and well-being stronger.

The next chapters will guide you through easy steps, learned from my experiences, to handle things better. From setting clear boundaries to talking openly with your spouse, these strategies will help turn a tough situation into a source of strength. As we go through this journey together, my goal is to give you hope and practical help. I want these pages to be a guide for those facing a tricky relationship with their mother-in-law. I pray that you find encouragement, direction, and the power to not just get through it but to come out stronger and happier in your marital and family life.

CHAPTER 1: UNVEILING THE DYNAMICS

In family relationships, understanding the dynamics of dealing with a narcissistic mother-in-law is a crucial first step. This chapter delves into recognizing the distinctive traits of narcissism and the profound impact it can have on your marriage and family.

Recognizing Narcissistic Traits

Narcissistic traits often lurk beneath the surface, and learning to identify them is like deciphering a code. Recognizing narcissistic traits in a mother-in-law (or anyone else) can be challenging, as individuals may exhibit a range of behaviors that can be interpreted in various ways. It's important to note that only a qualified mental health professional can diagnose narcissistic personality disorder (NPD).

However, here are some common traits associated with narcissism that you may observe in a person, including a mother-in-law:

Lack of Empathy: She might often dismiss others' emotions or experiences or find difficulty understanding or caring about others' feelings and needs.

Exaggerated Sense of Self-Importance: She may display an excessive need for admiration, constant validation, and a tendency to overstate achievements and talents.

Manipulative Behavior: You might see her using others for personal gain or to achieve their own goals, or she tends to exploit or take advantage of relationships.

Sense of Entitlement: Narcissistic mothers-in-law often believe they deserve special treatment or recognition without necessarily earning it and also expect others to comply with their wishes.

Difficulty with Criticism: They often react strongly to criticism, become defensive or hostile, and refuse to accept responsibility for mistakes.

Boundary Violation: You might also notice a lack of respect for others' boundaries and a tendency to invade personal space.

Pattern of Controlling Behavior: She might also display an inclination to control or dominate conversations and decision-making or a need to be in control of various aspects of others' lives.

Lack of Genuine Interest in Others: You might also notice that she finds it difficult to form deep, meaningful connections. They often possess superficial relationships, with a focus on how others can serve their needs.

It's important to approach these observations with care and avoid jumping to conclusions. People may exhibit certain traits from time to time without having a personality disorder. By unraveling these behaviors, you gain a clearer understanding of the challenges ahead. Recognizing narcissistic traits is not about labeling or blaming but about acknowledging patterns of behavior that can strain relationships. This awareness forms the foundation for crafting strategies to navigate through the complexities with grace and resilience.

Impact on Marriage and Family

The ripple effect of a narcissistic mother-in-law extends far beyond individual interactions. It weaves its way into the fabric of your marriage and family life, leaving lasting impressions and requiring intentional navigation.

In my marriage, I felt the impact in the form of increased stress, communication breakdowns, and potential and unnecessary conflicts with my spouse. The constant juggling act to meet the demands and expectations of both my spouse and my mother-in-law can create a challenging balancing act, often leading to emotional fatigue. Within the broader family context, the influence of a narcissistic figure can disrupt the harmonious flow of the home.

Sibling relationships may be strained, and children might find themselves caught in the crossfire of conflicting expectations and behaviors. The atmosphere within your home may become tense, affecting the overall emotional well-being of everyone involved. Understanding the specific ways in which a narcissistic mother-in-law affects your marriage and family allows you to address these challenges more effectively. It's about recognizing patterns of behavior that create tension and finding strategies to mitigate their impact, fostering a healthier and more resilient family dynamic.

The chapters ahead aim to shine a light on these dynamics, offering a roadmap for navigating these complexities. By understanding the traits of narcissism and recognizing their effects on your marriage and family, you lay the groundwork for the transformative journey outlined in the chapters that follow. The goal is to emerge stronger, fostering a home environment that thrives despite the presence of narcissistic dynamics.

CHAPTER 2: EMOTIONAL DETOXIFICATION

In the rollercoaster of relationships, emotional detoxification becomes a vital checkpoint, especially when dealing with a challenging mother-in-law. This chapter delves into coping mechanisms for emotional well-being and explores the art of letting go of negative energy to create a healthier, more resilient emotional landscape.

Coping Mechanisms for Emotional Well-Being

The emotional toll of navigating a relationship with a narcissistic mother-in-law can be significant. Emotional detox involves adopting coping mechanisms to navigate the complexities while safeguarding your mental and emotional health.

Mindfulness and Presence: Embrace mindfulness techniques to stay present in the moment. Grounding yourself in the present and now can reduce anxiety and prevent emotional overwhelm.

Journaling: Expressing your feelings through journaling provides an outlet for pent-up emotions. It allows you to reflect on your experiences and gain clarity on your emotional state.

Healthy Outlets for Stress: Engage in activities that alleviate stress, such as exercise, art, or spending time in nature. These activities serve as constructive outlets for negative energy.

Therapeutic Support: Consider seeking therapy to navigate complex emotions. A trained therapist can provide guidance, offer coping strategies, and serve as a neutral sounding board.

Positive Affirmations: Counteract negative thoughts with positive affirmations. Remind yourself of your strengths, achievements, and the value you bring to your relationships.

Create Emotional Boundaries: Establish clear emotional boundaries to protect yourself from absorbing negativity. Recognize when to disengage emotionally and focus on preserving your own well-being.

Limit Exposure to Negativity: Set limits on exposure to negative influences, whether through minimizing contact or creating physical and emotional distance when necessary.

Practice Self-compassion: Acknowledge that dealing with a challenging mother-in-law is difficult, so treat yourself with kindness and understanding, and it's okay to prioritize your emotional well-being.

Build a Support System: Surround yourself with a supportive network of friends and family who understand your experiences. Sharing your feelings with trusted individuals can be a powerful source of comfort.

Educate Yourself: Knowledge is empowering, understanding the dynamics of narcissism can demystify challenging behaviors and help you navigate them with a clearer perspective.

Letting Go of Negative Energy

Letting go of negative energy is an essential aspect of emotional detox. It involves releasing the grip of resentment, frustration, and hurt that may accumulate in the wake of interactions with a difficult mother-in-law.

Forgiveness: Practice forgiveness, not for the sake of the other person but for your own peace of mind. Letting go of grudges frees you from the emotional burden.

Detach from the Outcome: Accept that you cannot control or change the behavior of your mother-in-law. Detach from the expectation of a specific outcome and focus on your own emotional well-being.

Cultivate Gratitude: Shift your focus towards gratitude. Recognize positive aspects in your life, fostering a mindset that can counterbalance the negativity.

Release Guilt: Understand that setting boundaries and prioritizing your well-being is not selfish. Release any guilt associated with prioritizing your emotional health.

Visualization Techniques: Use visualization to release negative energy. Imagine letting go of toxic emotions, allowing them to dissipate like leaves carried away by a gentle breeze.

Engage in Relaxation Techniques: Practices such as deep breathing, meditation, or progressive muscle relaxation can help release tension and negative energy.

Create a Positive Environment: Surround yourself with positivity. Arrange your physical space and engage in activities that uplift your mood and create a more positive atmosphere.

Learn from Experiences: Instead of dwelling on negative encounters, view them as opportunities for growth and learning. Extract lessons that contribute to your emotional resilience.

By incorporating coping mechanisms for emotional well-being and mastering the art of letting go of negative energy, you empower yourself to navigate the challenges of a relationship with a narcissistic mother-in-law with grace and resilience.

CHAPTER 3: OPEN COMMUNICATION

Open communication is the cornerstone of navigating the dynamics of a relationship with a narcissistic mother-in-law. This chapter delves into the importance of transparent communication, providing insights into navigating conversations with your spouse and communicating effectively with your mother-in-law.

Navigating Conversations with a Spouse

A strong partnership with your spouse is the linchpin for successfully navigating the challenges posed by a narcissistic mother-in-law. Transparent communication with your spouse is essential for fostering unity and resilience.

Create a Safe Space: Establish an environment where both partners feel safe expressing their thoughts and feelings without fear of judgment. This creates a foundation for open and honest communication.

Active Listening: Practice active listening when your spouse shares their experiences and concerns. Validate their emotions and demonstrate empathy to strengthen your connection.

Express Your Needs Clearly: Clearly articulate your needs and boundaries, ensuring your spouse understands the specific challenges you face in the relationship with your mother-in-law.

Joint Decision-Making: Collaborate on decisions related to interactions with your mother-in-law. Joint decision-making reinforces the unity of your partnership and minimizes potential conflicts.

Regular Check-Ins: Schedule regular check-ins to discuss how you both are coping with the challenges. This ongoing dialogue allows for mutual support and the adjustment of strategies as needed.

Seek Professional Guidance: If communication becomes challenging, consider seeking professional guidance through couples therapy. A therapist can provide tools and strategies to enhance communication and strengthen your partnership.

Communicating Effectively with Mother-in-Law

Effectively communicating with a narcissistic mother-in-law requires a strategic and empathetic approach. These techniques can help navigate conversations while minimizing conflict.

Stay Calm and Collected: Maintain composure during conversations, avoiding the escalation of emotions. A calm demeanor can diffuse tension and create a more conducive environment for communication.

Use "I" Statements: Express your feelings using "I" statements to avoid sounding accusatory. For example, say "I feel" instead of "You always." This fosters a more open and less confrontational dialogue.

Establish Clear Boundaries: Reiterate and reinforce established boundaries during conversations. Clearly communicate the expectations you have for respectful and healthy interactions.

Choose Your Battles: Prioritize issues that truly matter and let go of minor conflicts. Being selective in your engagement will help conserve emotional energy for more critical situations.

Set Realistic Expectations: Understand that change may be gradual. Set realistic expectations for your interactions, acknowledging that certain behaviors may persist but that your responses can evolve.

Use Empathy as a Tool: Approach conversations with empathy, trying to understand her perspective. This doesn't mean accepting negative behavior, but rather creating a space for more constructive dialogue.

Redirect Negative Energy: When faced with negativity, redirect the conversation toward neutral or positive topics. Steering discussions away from conflict-prone areas helps maintain a more harmonious atmosphere.

Establish Consequences: Clearly communicate consequences for disrespectful behavior. Whether it's limiting contact or taking a break from interactions, establish repercussions to reinforce boundaries.

Involve Your Spouse as a Support: When necessary, involve your spouse in conversations. Having a supportive partner present can reinforce your boundaries and provide an additional layer of accountability.

Know When to Disengage: Recognize when a conversation is unproductive or escalating. It's okay to disengage and revisit the discussion at a later, more opportune time.

By mastering the art of open communication with your spouse and developing effective strategies for conversing with your mother-in-law, you empower yourself to navigate the intricate dynamics of these relationships.

CHAPTER 4: SETTING BOUNDARIES

In familial relationships, the concept of setting boundaries emerges as a powerful tool for navigating the challenges posed by a narcissistic mother-in-law. This chapter dives into the significance of establishing boundaries and provides practical strategies for their effective implementation.

Importance of Boundaries

Boundaries are the invisible lines that define the space between individuals, dictating what is acceptable and what is not. In the context of dealing with a narcissistic mother-in-law, establishing clear boundaries is akin to creating a protective shield for your emotional well-being and the harmony of your marriage. Narcissistic individuals often push against boundaries, testing limits to see how much they can influence and control.

Without well-defined boundaries, the potential for emotional manipulation and turmoil escalates. Recognizing the importance of setting boundaries is the first step toward reclaiming control over your personal space and relationships. Boundaries serve as a safeguard, preserving your mental and emotional health while creating a framework for healthy interactions. They communicate expectations and establish a baseline of respect, offering a roadmap for navigating the complexities of a relationship with a challenging mother-in-law.

Practical Strategies for Implementation

Implementing boundaries may seem daunting, but it is a vital aspect of creating a healthy dynamic with a narcissistic mother-in-law. Here are practical strategies to guide you through this process:

- **Self-Reflection:** Before setting boundaries, take some time to reflect on your own needs, values, and limits. Understanding your own boundaries empowers you to communicate them more effectively.

- **Clear Communication:** Express your boundaries with clarity and assertiveness. Use "I" statements to convey your feelings and needs, focusing on your perspective rather than placing blame. For example, "I feel uncomfortable when..."

- **Consistency is important:** Consistency reinforces the message of your boundaries. Be firm and unwavering in upholding them, as inconsistency may be perceived as an invitation for manipulation.

- **Establish Consequences:** Clearly communicate the consequences of crossing established boundaries. This may involve limiting contact, taking a break from interactions, or seeking support from your spouse.

- **Involve Your Spouse:** Work as a team with your spouse to set and enforce boundaries. A united front sends a strong message and reinforces the importance of respecting these limits.

- **Prioritize Self-Care:** Setting boundaries is an act of self-care. Prioritize your mental and emotional well-being by enforcing the boundaries that protect your peace of mind.

- **Seek External Support:** If necessary, involve a trusted friend, family member, or therapist to provide additional support and guidance in establishing and maintaining boundaries.

- **Adapt and re-evaluate:** As circumstances change, be open to adapting your boundaries. Regularly reassess and refine them based on evolving needs and experiences.

- **Educate yourself:** Learn more about narcissistic behaviors to better anticipate potential challenges and adjust your boundaries accordingly. Knowledge is a powerful tool for navigating these complex dynamics.

- **Celebrate Success:** Acknowledge and celebrate moments when your boundaries are respected. Positive reinforcement encourages both you and your mother-in-law to understand and respect each other's limits.

By integrating these practical strategies, you have embarked on a journey of self-empowerment and relationship resilience. Setting boundaries is not a sign of weakness but a proactive measure to foster a healthier, more harmonious connection with your mother-in-law and safeguard the well-being of your marriage. In the chapters that follow, we'll continue exploring transformative approaches to navigate the intricate dynamics of dealing with a narcissistic mother-in-law.

CHAPTER 5: CULTIVATING EMPATHY

Cultivating empathy emerges as a potent tool for transforming the dynamics with a narcissistic mother-in-law. This chapter delves into the importance of understanding the root causes of her behavior and provides insights into developing empathy in challenging situations.

Understanding the Root Causes

To cultivate empathy, it's crucial to unravel the layers that shroud the behavior of a narcissistic mother-in-law. Understanding the root causes provides a nuanced perspective, shedding light on the underlying factors that contribute to her actions.

- **Past Experiences:** Consider the possibility that past experiences may have shaped her behavior. Empathy involves acknowledging that personal histories, whether filled with trauma or challenges, can significantly impact one's approach to relationships.

- **Insecurity and Fear:** Narcissistic behaviors often stem from deep-seated insecurities and fear. By recognizing these vulnerabilities, you can empathize with the defensive mechanisms she employs to protect herself from perceived threats.

- **Lack of Emotional Regulation:** A narcissistic individual may struggle with emotional regulation, leading to outbursts or manipulative tactics. Understanding this challenge allows you to approach situations with a compassionate lens, recognizing it as a coping mechanism.

- **Seeking Validation:** Consider the possibility that her actions are rooted in a persistent need for validation. Empathy involves understanding that beneath the surface bravado lies a yearning for acknowledgment and approval.

- **Limited Coping Strategies:** A narcissistic mother-in-law may possess limited coping strategies for handling stress or conflicts. Viewing her actions through this lens allows for a more empathetic understanding of her struggle to navigate challenging situations.

Developing Empathy in Challenging Situations

Empathy is a learned skill that can be honed even in the face of challenging relationships. Here are strategies to develop empathy when dealing with a narcissistic mother-in-law:

- **Active Listening:** Practice active listening to truly understand her perspective. Allow her to express herself without interruption, demonstrating that you are open to hearing her thoughts and feelings.

- **Put Yourself in Her Shoes:** Challenge yourself to imagine the world from her viewpoint. Consider her life experiences, fears, and insecurities, fostering a deeper understanding of the factors influencing her behavior.

- **Separate Behavior from Person:** Differentiate between her actions and her intrinsic worth as a person. Recognize that negative behaviors may be coping mechanisms and not a reflection of her entire identity.

- **Recognize Patterns**: Identify patterns in her behavior to discern triggers and stressors. This understanding enables you to anticipate potential challenges and respond with empathy rather than frustration.

- **Acknowledge Small Positive Actions:** Recognize and appreciate any positive actions or changes in behavior. Acknowledging even small steps fosters a more positive atmosphere and encourages further growth.

- **Seek Common Ground:** Identify shared interests or values that can serve as common ground. Finding areas of agreement can create bridges for more positive interactions.

- **Establish Clear Communication:** Openly communicate your feelings and needs while actively encouraging her to share hers. This reciprocal exchange fosters an environment of understanding and empathy.

- **Practice Patience:** Cultivating empathy requires patience. Understand that transformation is a gradual process, and consistent effort is key to fostering positive change.

- **Educate Yourself:** Learn more about narcissistic personality traits and behaviors. Knowledge is a powerful tool that can demystify challenging actions and contribute to a more empathetic approach.

- **Set Boundaries with Empathy:** When establishing or reinforcing boundaries, do so with empathy. Communicate your needs clearly while acknowledging the challenges she may face in adjusting to these limits.

Cultivating empathy is not about condoning negative behavior but rather about fostering a deeper understanding that can lead to more compassionate and constructive interactions. By peeling back the layers and developing empathy in challenging situations, you set the stage for transformative growth, both in your relationship with your mother-in-law and within yourself. In the chapters that follow, we'll continue exploring strategies to navigate these intricate dynamics with grace and resilience.

CHAPTER 6: SELF-CARE RITUALS

Amidst the complexities of navigating a relationship with a narcissistic mother-in-law, the chapter on self-care rituals emerges as a sanctuary for your emotional well-being. This segment delves into the importance of prioritizing self-care, offering insights into creating a personal wellness plan that becomes a beacon of resilience in challenging times.

Prioritizing Self-Care

Self-care is not a luxury; it is a necessity, especially when dealing with challenging dynamics. Prioritizing self-care is akin to replenishing your emotional reserves, enabling you to face the complexities with renewed vigor.

Recognize the Need for Self-Care: Acknowledge when you need a break. Recognizing the signs of emotional fatigue allows you to intervene with self-care measures before reaching a point of burnout.

Guilt-Free Self-Care: Release any guilt associated with taking time for yourself. Self-care is not selfish; it is a fundamental aspect of maintaining your mental and emotional health.

Understand Individual Needs: Self-care is highly individualistic. Understand what activities or practices rejuvenate you personally, whether it's reading, exercise, meditation, or simply enjoying quiet moments.

Regular Check-Ins with Yourself: Conduct regular check-ins with your emotional well-being. Assess how you are feeling and identify areas where self-care may be particularly beneficial.

Set Boundaries: Establish clear boundaries around your personal time. Communicate these boundaries to your spouse and other family members, emphasizing the importance of respecting your need for self-care.

Incorporate Daily Rituals: Integrate small, daily rituals into your routine. These can be brief moments of mindfulness, a short walk, or a few minutes of dedicated relaxation to break up the day.

Quality Sleep: Prioritize quality sleep as a form of self-care. Ensure you are getting enough rest to support your physical and emotional well-being.

Balancing Responsibilities: Strive for a balance between your responsibilities and self-care. It's essential to fulfill your roles, but not at the expense of neglecting your own needs.

Creating a Personal Wellness Plan

A personalized wellness plan serves as a roadmap for prioritizing self-care. Tailor these elements to your preferences and needs, ensuring a holistic approach to well-being.

Physical Well-Being: Incorporate physical activities that bring joy and relaxation. Whether it's yoga, jogging, or dancing, find what resonates with you. Physical well-being is integral to overall health.

Mindfulness Practices: Integrate mindfulness practices into your routine. This could include meditation, deep breathing exercises, or moments of quiet reflection. These practices foster mental clarity and resilience.

Creative Outlets: Engage in creative pursuits that bring fulfillment. Whether it's painting, writing, or playing a musical instrument, these outlets provide an emotional release and a sense of accomplishment.

Social Connections: Foster positive social connections. Surround yourself with friends and family who uplift and support you.

Quality relationships contribute significantly to emotional well-being.

Alone Time: Carve out moments of solitude. Alone time allows for introspection and recharge, particularly important when navigating challenging relationships.

Technology Detox: Implement periodic technology detoxes. Disconnecting from digital devices can alleviate stress and create a more serene environment.

Healthy Nutrition: Prioritize a balanced and nourishing diet. Nutrient-rich foods contribute not only to physical health but also to emotional well-being.

Regular Health Check-Ups: Schedule regular health check-ups. Proactive health management is a crucial aspect of overall wellness.

Therapeutic Support: Consider therapy or counseling as part of your wellness plan. Professional support can offer valuable tools for coping with challenges and enhancing resilience.

Adaptability and Flexibility: Maintain flexibility in your wellness plan. Life is dynamic, and adapting your self-care practices to changing circumstances ensures ongoing effectiveness.

By prioritizing self-care and crafting a personalized wellness plan, you fortify yourself against the emotional toll of dealing with a challenging mother-in-law. This chapter encourages you to view self-care not as a luxury but as a fundamental investment in your resilience and well-being. In the upcoming chapters, we'll continue exploring transformative strategies to navigate the intricate dynamics with grace and strength.

CHAPTER 7: UNIFIED FRONT

This chapter is about presenting a unified front with your spouse, which emerges as a pivotal force when dealing with a narcissistic mother-in-law. This segment delves into the importance of strengthening the partnership with your spouse and the transformative power of presenting a united front.

Strengthening Partnership with Spouse

A resilient partnership forms the bedrock for navigating the challenges posed by a narcissistic mother-in-law. Strengthening this partnership involves intentional efforts to foster understanding, support, and unity.

Open Dialogue: Cultivate open dialogue with your spouse by encouraging honest conversations about your experiences, emotions, and perspectives. Transparency lays the foundation for mutual understanding.

Active Listening: Create a space where both partners feel heard and validated. This mutual exchange of understanding enhances emotional connection and solidarity.

Empathy for Each Other's Perspectives: Develop empathy for each other's perspectives, recognize that both of you may face unique challenges in dealing with the mother-in-law, and foster mutual support.

Shared Goals and Values: Clarify shared goals and values. Aligning your aspirations creates a unified vision for your family, reinforcing the strength of your partnership.

Respect for Individual Boundaries: Acknowledge that each person may have different ways of coping and establish an environment that supports both individuals. Respect individual boundaries within the partnership.

Regular Check-Ins: Schedule regular check-ins to discuss your experiences and feelings, as these check-ins serve as proactive measures to address any emerging challenges and reinforce your connection.

Presenting a United Front

Presenting a united front is a strategic approach to dealing with a challenging mother-in-law. It communicates solidarity and sets clear expectations for respectful interactions.

Joint Decision-Making: Engage in joint decision-making regarding interactions with your mother-in-law. Presenting a united front in decisions reinforces the partnership and sends a clear message of cohesion.

Consistent Messaging: Maintain consistency in your messaging, whether setting boundaries or addressing challenging behaviors; consistency reinforces the strength of your united front.

Agreed-Upon Boundaries: Establish agreed-upon boundaries and communicate them jointly. A unified presentation of expectations leaves little room for manipulation and reinforces the importance of respecting limits.

Mutual Support in Confrontations: When faced with challenging situations, offer mutual support during confrontations. Presenting a united front during interactions communicates that your partnership is unwavering.

Private Discussions: Reserve more sensitive discussions for private settings, addressing concerns privately to allow for candid conversations without undermining the unified front presented in public.

Recognize Each Other's Strengths: Acknowledge and appreciate each other's strengths. Recognizing the unique contributions each partner brings to the partnership reinforces the strength of your united front.

Balanced Division of Responsibilities: Distribute responsibilities in dealing with the mother-in-law in a balanced way. A united front is maintained when both partners actively contribute to managing interactions and challenges.

Avoiding Blame Games: Refrain from blaming each other in challenging situations; a united front involves facing challenges as a team, focusing on solutions rather than assigning blame.

Professional Guidance Together: If needed, seek professional guidance together. Couples therapy can offer tools and strategies for presenting a united front while navigating the complexities of a challenging relationship.

Celebrate Joint Successes: Celebrate successes as a team by acknowledging and reinforcing positive interactions or milestones achieved in presenting a united front, fostering a sense of accomplishment and shared resilience.

Presenting a united front is not about masking differences but about navigating challenges together with a shared commitment. This chapter encourages you to view your partnership as a source of strength, emphasizing the transformative impact it can have on the dynamics of a narcissistic mother-in-law.

CHAPTER 8: SELECTIVE ENGAGEMENT

In managing relationships, the chapter on selective engagement becomes a strategic guide when dealing with a narcissistic mother-in-law. This segment explores the art of choosing battles wisely and knowing when to disengage for the sake of preserving your emotional well-being.

Choosing Battles Wisely

Confrontations with a narcissistic mother-in-law can feel like navigating a minefield, but not every battle needs to be fought. Choosing battles wisely is an art that involves discernment, strategic thinking, and a focus on long-term harmony.

Prioritize Essential Issues: Identify and prioritize issues that are essential for the well-being of your marriage and family. Reserve your energy for matters that significantly impact your relationships or personal boundaries.

Assess the Long-Term Impact: Consider the long-term impact of engaging in a particular battle. Will it contribute positively to your well-being or relationship, or is it a momentary challenge that can be overlooked?

Evaluate Emotional Investment: Assess the emotional investment required for a particular confrontation. Some battles may drain your emotional reserves without yielding significant benefits.

Strategic Timing: Choose the timing of your battles strategically. Timing can influence the outcome, and addressing issues when emotions are less heightened may lead to more constructive discussions.

Consider the source: Evaluate the source of the conflict. Is it a recurring pattern of behavior or a one-time occurrence? Knowing the source helps in determining whether it's worth engaging in a battle.

Focus on Solutions, Not Blame: Shift the focus from blaming to finding solutions. Battles centered on blaming often lead to escalation, while those focused on solutions contribute to resolution.

Maintain Flexibility: Be flexible in your approach. Sometimes, adapting to the situation rather than engaging in a direct confrontation can lead to more favorable outcomes.

Anticipate Manipulative Tactics: Be aware of potential manipulative tactics. Narcissistic individuals may employ various strategies to divert attention or shift blame. Anticipating these tactics helps you stay focused on the core issue.

Involve your Spouse in Decision-Making: Consult your spouse before engaging in a battle. A united front strengthens your position, and involving your spouse ensures you are both aligned in choosing which battles to address.

Learn from Past Experiences: Reflect on past experiences. What battles have yielded positive results, and which ones have been counterproductive? Learning from history guides your approach to future engagements.

Knowing When to Disengage

Equally crucial to selective engagement is the ability to recognize when it's time to disengage. Disengagement is not a sign of weakness; it's a strategic move to protect your well-being and maintain a sense of balance.

Recognize Escalation: Pay attention to signs of escalation. In instances where a situation is spiraling into increased tension and conflict, disengagement can prevent further damage.

Emotional Exhaustion: Acknowledge that emotional exhaustion when engaging in a battle is depleting your emotional reserves with little positive outcome. Disengaging becomes a necessary act of self-preservation.

Respect Your Boundaries: If a situation is pushing against your established boundaries, disengaging reinforces the importance of respecting those limits. Know when to prioritize your boundaries.

Assess the Impact on Mental Health: Assess the impact on your mental health. If a battle is significantly affecting your well-being, disengaging allows you to prioritize your mental health.

Redirect Focus: Instead of dwelling on the conflict, shift your attention to activities or thoughts that bring positivity and peace. Redirect your focus when battles become unproductive.

Create Physical Distance: Create physical distance when needed. Sometimes, a brief break from a challenging situation provides the perspective needed to approach it more effectively later.

Seek Support: If disengagement is challenging, seek support from friends, family, or a therapist. Having a support system reinforces your decision and provides guidance on navigating difficult situations.

Avoid Being Pulled into Drama: Resist being pulled into unnecessary drama. Narcissistic individuals may thrive on creating chaos; disengaging denies them the opportunity to escalate conflicts.

Set Clear Communication: Establish clear communication about your decision to disengage. Clearly convey your need for space or time to revisit the conversation at a more opportune moment.

Focus on Self-Care: Use the time of disengagement for self-care. Prioritize activities that bring you joy, relaxation, and rejuvenation, reinforcing the importance of your well-being.

By mastering the art of selective engagement and knowing when to disengage, you empower yourself to navigate the challenges of a relationship with a narcissistic mother-in-law strategically. This chapter encourages you to approach conflicts with discernment, prioritizing your emotional well-being and long-term harmony. In the chapters that follow, we'll continue exploring transformative strategies to foster resilience and strength in navigating these intricate dynamics.

CHAPTER 9: BUILDING SUPPORT NETWORKS

In managing relationships, the chapter on building support networks emerges as a lifeline when dealing with a narcissistic mother-in-law. This segment explores the significance of seeking support from friends and family, as well as the transformative potential of professional guidance and therapy.

Seeking Support from Friends and Family

Building a robust support network involves reaching out to friends and family who can offer understanding, empathy, and a sense of connection. Navigating the challenges posed by a narcissistic mother-in-law becomes more manageable when shared with those who genuinely care about your well-being.

Identify Trustworthy Allies: Identify friends and family members whom you trust and feel comfortable confiding in. These individuals can serve as reliable allies in times of emotional distress.

Open Communication: Foster open communication with your support network. Clearly express your feelings and experiences, helping them understand the nuances of your relationship with your mother-in-law.

Set Boundaries with Your Support System: Establish boundaries with your support system by clearly communicating what you need from them, whether it's a listening ear, advice, or occasional respite from challenging situations.

Celebrate Positive Moments: Share positive moments with them as well. Celebrate milestones and successes in navigating challenges. Positive reinforcement creates a supportive atmosphere within your network.

Plan Regular Check-Ins: Plan your regular check-ins with your support system. These check-ins provide opportunities to share updates, seek advice, and receive emotional support.

Avoid Negative Influence: Be mindful of potential negative influence. Surround yourself with individuals who uplift and support you rather than those who may inadvertently contribute to increased stress.

Share Educational Resources: Share educational resources on narcissism with your support network. Providing insights into the dynamics you are facing can enhance understanding and empathy.

Encourage Honest Feedback: Encourage honest feedback from your support system. Constructive feedback can offer valuable perspectives and potential solutions to navigate challenges.

Express Gratitude: Express gratitude for their support. A simple acknowledgment of the impact their support has on your well-being strengthens the bonds within your support network.

Respect Their Boundaries: Respect the boundaries of your support system. Understand that not everyone may be equipped to provide the same level of support, and that's okay.

Professional Guidance and Therapy

Sometimes, the complexities of dealing with a narcissistic mother-in-law may necessitate professional guidance. Therapy offers a structured and confidential space to explore challenges, gain insights, and develop effective coping strategies.

Individual Therapy: A therapist provides a safe and non-judgmental environment for you to explore your thoughts and emotions, offering guidance on personal growth and coping mechanisms so consider individual therapy.

Couples Therapy: Explore couples therapy with your spouse as it can facilitate constructive communication, assist in setting joint goals, and offer strategies for navigating challenges as a united front.

Family Therapy: Family therapy may be beneficial for addressing broader family dynamics. This form of therapy explores relationships and communication patterns, fostering a more harmonious family environment.

Therapeutic Techniques for Coping: Learn therapeutic techniques for coping with stress and emotional challenges. Therapists often provide practical tools that can be applied in daily life to enhance resilience.

Navigate Emotional Triggers: Therapists help you navigate emotional triggers related to the narcissistic behavior. Understanding and managing these triggers is essential for emotional well-being.

Receive Validation and Understanding: Therapy offers validation and understanding. Having a professional acknowledge the challenges you face can be profoundly affirming, contributing to a sense of empowerment.

Develop Healthy Coping Mechanisms: Work with a therapist to develop healthy coping mechanisms. These strategies empower you to respond to challenging situations in ways that align with your well-being.

Set Realistic Expectations: Therapists assist in setting realistic expectations. A clearer understanding of what can be achieved in challenging relationships supports a more grounded and resilient approach.

Explore Boundary Setting: Explore effective boundary-setting strategies. Therapists can guide you in establishing and maintaining boundaries that protect your mental and emotional health.

Support during Decision-Making: Seek support during decision-making. Therapists offer insights and guidance as you navigate choices related to your relationship with your mother-in-law.

Building a support network that includes friends and family, as well as professional guidance through therapy, creates a comprehensive and empowering foundation for navigating the complexities of dealing with a narcissistic mother-in-law. In the chapters that follow, we'll continue exploring transformative strategies to foster resilience and strength in these intricate dynamics.

CHAPTER 10: CELEBRATING DIFFERENCES

This chapter on celebrating differences becomes a beacon of unity when dealing with a narcissistic mother-in-law. This segment explores the transformative power of embracing diversity in perspectives and the art of finding common ground within the family unit.

Embracing Diversity in Perspectives

Every individual brings a unique set of experiences, values, and perspectives to the family dynamic. Embracing this diversity is not just a path to harmony; it's a celebration of the richness that each member contributes. When faced with a narcissistic mother-in-law, the ability to appreciate differences becomes a cornerstone for fostering resilience.

Acknowledge Individual Identities: Acknowledge and celebrate the individual identities within the family. Recognize that each person, including your mother-in-law, is shaped by a unique combination of experiences, beliefs, and aspirations.

Understand Generational Differences: Generational differences often play a significant role. Recognize that your mother-in-law may come from a different era with distinct values and societal norms. Understanding these differences fosters empathy.

Cultivate Open-Mindedness: Cultivate open-mindedness within the family. Embrace the idea that diverse perspectives contribute to a more enriched family environment, fostering creativity and adaptability.

Value Different Communication Styles: Individuals may have different communication styles. Some may be more direct, while others prefer subtlety. Appreciate and adapt to these differences to enhance effective communication.

Explore Cultural Variances: Explore cultural variances that may influence perspectives. If your mother-in-law comes from a different cultural background, understanding these influences can provide valuable insights into her worldview.

Encourage Expressing Individual Opinions: Create an atmosphere where individuals feel comfortable expressing their opinions. This encourages open communication and helps prevent the suppression of diverse perspectives.

Celebrate Personal Achievements: Celebrate personal achievements within the family. Whether it's academic accomplishments, career milestones, or personal growth, acknowledging and celebrating individual successes reinforces a positive family culture.

Practice Empathy: Practice empathy in understanding differing viewpoints. Empathy involves putting yourself in another's shoes, fostering compassion even when perspectives diverge.

Learn from Each Other: Embrace the opportunity to learn from each other. Everyone, including your mother-in-law, brings unique skills, knowledge, and experiences that can contribute to the collective wisdom of the family.

Create Inclusive Family Traditions: Establish inclusive family traditions that honor diverse backgrounds and preferences. This fosters a sense of belonging and unity within the family.

Finding Common Ground

While celebrating differences is crucial, finding common ground acts as the glue that binds the family together. Identifying shared values, interests, and goals creates a foundation for unity, even in the face of challenging dynamics.

Identify Shared Values: Identify and emphasize shared values within the family. These shared principles become touchstones that guide decision-making and behavior, fostering a sense of unity.

Discover Common Interests: Discover and nurture common interests. Whether it's a shared hobby, passion, or recreational activity, finding common ground creates opportunities for positive interactions.

Establish Common Goals: Establish common goals for the family. These goals can be related to personal growth, mutual support, or shared achievements that contribute to the well-being of each family member.

Joint Family Projects: Engage in joint family projects. Collaborative efforts, whether it's a home improvement task or planning a family event, strengthen bonds and provide a sense of shared purpose.

Celebrate Shared Milestones: Celebrate shared milestones and achievements. Recognizing collective successes reinforces the idea that the family is a united entity, capable of overcoming challenges together.

Encourage Collaboration: Encourage collaboration in decision-making. In situations involving your mother-in-law, collaborative decision-making reinforces the importance of unity and shared responsibility.

Facilitate Family Discussions: Facilitate family discussions on important topics. Open dialogue creates opportunities to find common ground and understand each other's perspectives.

Prioritize Family Time: Prioritize dedicated family time. Whether it's regular dinners, outings, or vacations, intentional family time fosters connections and reinforces the importance of the family unit.

Create Inclusive Family Traditions: Inclusive family traditions also play a role in finding common ground. Traditions that resonate with everyone create a sense of continuity and shared identity.

Foster a Culture of Mutual Respect: Above all, foster a culture of mutual respect. Respect for each family member's individuality and perspectives forms the bedrock for finding common ground and maintaining family harmony.

In navigating the complexities of dealing with a narcissistic mother-in-law, the chapter on celebrating differences and finding common ground underscores the importance of unity within the family. Embracing diversity and identifying shared values contribute to a resilient family unit capable of withstanding challenges with grace and strength. As we delve into the final chapters, we'll continue exploring transformative strategies to foster resilience and harmony in navigating these intricate dynamics.

CHAPTER 11: POSITIVE REINFORCEMENT

In the intricate tapestry of family dynamics, the chapter on positive reinforcement emerges as a powerful tool when dealing with a narcissistic mother-in-law. This segment explores the transformative impact of acknowledging and encouraging positive behavior, fostering a foundation of constructive relationships within the family unit.

Acknowledging and Encouraging Positive Behavior

Positive reinforcement operates as a catalyst for change, creating an environment that encourages constructive interactions. When navigating the complexities of a relationship with a narcissistic mother-in-law, intentionally acknowledging and encouraging positive behavior becomes a key strategy.

Identify and Acknowledge Efforts: Actively identify and acknowledge positive efforts made by your mother-in-law. This recognition serves as a powerful motivator, reinforcing the idea that positive behavior is noticed and appreciated.

Express Genuine Appreciation: Express genuine appreciation for positive actions. Be specific in your praise, highlighting the particular behavior or effort that you find commendable.

Reinforce Positive Intentions: Reinforce positive intentions. When your mother-in-law demonstrates a genuine desire to contribute positively, acknowledging her intentions reinforces the importance of fostering goodwill.

Use Positive Language: Utilize positive language when providing feedback. Framing your observations in a positive light encourages a receptive and open response.

Create a Culture of Positivity: Strive to create a culture of positivity within the family. Encourage family members, including your mother-in-law, to focus on uplifting and affirming interactions.

Model Positive Behavior: Lead by example. Model the positive behavior you wish to see within the family, demonstrating the impact of constructive interactions.

Celebrate Milestones: Celebrate milestones and positive changes. Whether it's a shift in behavior, improved communication, or collaborative efforts, recognizing these milestones reinforces the value of positive growth.

Encourage Communication Skills: If there are improvements in communication skills, encourage and acknowledge them. Effective communication is foundational to constructive relationships, and positive reinforcement reinforces its importance.

Provide Opportunities for Growth: Offer opportunities for personal and relational growth. When positive behavior is acknowledged, individuals are more likely to continue investing in constructive actions.

Incorporate Positive Reinforcement in Daily Interactions: Integrate positive reinforcement into daily interactions. Small, consistent acknowledgments of positive behavior contribute to an overall positive family atmosphere.

Reinforcing Constructive Relationships

Positive reinforcement extends beyond individual actions; it plays a pivotal role in reinforcing constructive relationships within the family unit. Building and maintaining healthy relationships, especially when dealing with a challenging dynamic, requires intentional efforts to nurture positivity.

Foster Mutual Respect: Emphasize and reinforce the importance of mutual respect. Positive reinforcement for respectful behavior contributes to the development of a culture of courtesy within the family.

Encourage Empathy: Acknowledge and encourage empathy. When family members, including your mother-in-law, demonstrate understanding and empathy, reinforcing these qualities strengthens interpersonal connections.

Promote Teamwork: Highlight and celebrate instances of teamwork. Positive reinforcement for collaborative efforts reinforces the idea that collective goals are achievable through mutual support.

Address and Resolve Conflicts Positively: When conflicts are addressed positively, provide acknowledgment. Reinforcing constructive conflict resolution methods contributes to a healthier family dynamic.

Create Shared Positive Experiences: Foster shared positive experiences. Whether through family activities, celebrations, or shared achievements, creating positive moments reinforces a sense of unity.

Encourage Open Communication: Positive reinforcement for open communication reinforces its value. When family members feel comfortable expressing themselves openly, it contributes to stronger and more resilient relationships.

Support Individual Growth: Acknowledge and support individual growth. Positive reinforcement for personal development reinforces the idea that each family member, including your mother-in-law, is valued for their unique contributions.

Celebrate Family Traditions: Celebrate family traditions positively. Traditions that are met with positive reinforcement become cherished rituals that strengthen family bonds.

Express Gratitude: Regularly express gratitude for positive contributions. Positive reinforcement through expressions of gratitude fosters an atmosphere of appreciation within the family.

Encourage a Culture of Positivity: Establish and encourage an overall culture of positivity within the family. When positivity is reinforced consistently, it becomes an integral part of the family's identity.

In navigating the intricate dynamics of a relationship with a narcissistic mother-in-law, positive reinforcement becomes a guiding force for transformation. By intentionally acknowledging and encouraging positive behavior, both at the individual and relational levels, you contribute to the creation of a family environment built on constructive relationships. As we approach the final chapters, we'll continue exploring transformative strategies to foster resilience and harmony in navigating these intricate dynamics.

CHAPTER 12: CONTINUOUS GROWTH

This chapter on continuous growth becomes the culmination of transformative strategies when navigating a relationship with a narcissistic mother-in-law. This segment explores the profound impact of embracing personal growth and the art of transforming challenges into opportunities, fostering resilience and harmony within the family unit.

Embracing Personal Growth

Personal growth is a dynamic and ongoing journey, especially in the face of challenging relationships. When dealing with a narcissistic mother-in-law, the path to continuous growth involves intentional self-reflection, learning, and adaptation.

Reflect on Personal Responses: Engage in reflective practices. Regularly assess your responses to challenging situations, recognizing areas for personal growth. Self-awareness forms the foundation for intentional change.

Seek Continuous Learning: Cultivate a mindset of continuous learning. Explore resources on interpersonal dynamics, communication skills, and emotional intelligence. A commitment to learning equips you with tools for navigating complexities.

Embrace Resilience: Embrace resilience as a key component of personal growth. Resilience allows you to bounce back from challenges, transforming setbacks into opportunities for strengthening your emotional well-being.

Cultivate Emotional Intelligence: Cultivate emotional intelligence. Develop an understanding of your own emotions and those of others. Emotional intelligence facilitates more empathetic and constructive interactions within the family.

Explore Therapeutic Support: If needed, continue exploring therapeutic support. A therapist can provide guidance for personal growth, offering insights into coping mechanisms and strategies for navigating challenging relationships.

Set Personal Goals: Set personal goals for growth. These goals can range from improving communication skills to enhancing emotional resilience. Clear objectives create a roadmap for your ongoing development.

Celebrate Small Achievements: Celebrate small achievements along the way. Acknowledging progress, no matter how incremental, reinforces a positive mindset and encourages continued growth.

Engage in Self-Reflection: Regularly engage in self-reflection. Create moments of introspection to assess your emotional responses, communication patterns, and overall well-being. Self-reflection is a powerful tool for personal insight.

Establish Healthy Boundaries: Strengthen your ability to establish and maintain healthy boundaries. Personal growth involves developing a firm yet compassionate approach to setting limits that protect your well-being.

Practice Self-Compassion: Practice self-compassion. Be kind to yourself during moments of challenge or setbacks. Recognize that personal growth is a journey, and self-compassion fosters resilience.

Transforming Challenges into Opportunities

Challenges within a family, particularly those arising from a narcissistic dynamic, present unique opportunities for transformation. Viewing challenges through a lens of growth enables you to navigate difficulties with resilience and cultivate positive change.

Extract Lessons from Challenges: Extract valuable lessons from challenges. Each difficulty presents an opportunity to learn more about yourself, your relationships, and effective strategies for managing complexities.

Identify Patterns for Change: Identify recurring patterns within challenges. Recognizing patterns allows you to implement targeted changes, transforming the way you respond to and navigate difficult situations.

Seek Solutions Rather Than Blame: Shift the focus from blame to solutions. When faced with challenges, seek constructive ways to address the underlying issues, fostering a problem-solving approach within the family.

Turn Conflict into Constructive Dialogue: Transform conflicts into opportunities for constructive dialogue. Instead of viewing conflict as a threat, approach it as a catalyst for open communication, understanding, and resolution.

Encourage Family Growth Through Challenges: Encourage family growth through challenges. Difficulties can serve as shared experiences that strengthen family bonds, provided they are navigated with patience, empathy, and a commitment to growth.

Utilize Challenges as Catalysts for Change: View challenges as catalysts for positive change. Each obstacle presents an opportunity to reassess, adapt, and implement transformative strategies within the family unit.

Develop Problem-Solving Skills: Develop and hone problem-solving skills. Challenges provide a canvas for applying creative and effective solutions, fostering a culture of adaptability within the family.

Build Resilience in the Face of Adversity: Cultivate resilience in the face of adversity. Challenges test your ability to bounce back and adapt. Embracing these tests as opportunities for resilience contributes to personal and familial strength.

Encourage Collective Learning: Encourage collective learning within the family. When challenges arise, approach them as opportunities for shared growth, where each family member contributes to the collective learning experience.

Celebrate Progress Amidst Challenges: Celebrate progress made amidst challenges. Acknowledge and reinforce positive changes, no matter how small, as a testament to the family's collective ability to overcome difficulties.

In navigating the intricate dynamics of a relationship with a narcissistic mother-in-law, the chapter on continuous growth encapsulates the essence of resilience, adaptability, and positive transformation. Embracing personal growth and viewing challenges as opportunities for change contribute to the ongoing evolution of the family unit. As we conclude this exploration, the transformative strategies presented serve as guiding principles for fostering resilience and harmony within the complexities of family relationships.

REFLECTIONS ON TRANSFORMATION, MOVING FORWARD WITH HARMONY

As we conclude this journey through the intricacies of navigating a relationship with a narcissistic mother-in-law, it's essential to reflect on the transformative strategies explored and consider the path forward towards fostering harmony within the family unit. The journey of dealing with a challenging dynamic requires introspection, resilience, and a commitment to personal and collective growth. Each chapter has been a stepping stone, unveiling strategies that empower individuals to navigate complexities with grace. Reflection on these transformative principles unveils a mosaic of resilience, empathy, and positive change.

Throughout this exploration, empathy emerges as a transformative force. The ability to understand and share the feelings of both oneself and others lays the foundation for constructive relationships. Empathy becomes the bridge that fosters understanding even in the face of challenging dynamics while effective communication proves to be a linchpin in transforming relationships. Whether it's setting boundaries, engaging in open dialogue, or presenting a united front, communication becomes a tool for building bridges and fostering unity within the family.

The art of choosing battles wisely and knowing when to disengage emerges as a strategic approach. Selective engagement involves discernment, a focus on long-term harmony, and an understanding that not every conflict needs to be confronted. Knowing when to disengage becomes a skill that preserves emotional well-being. Remember the importance of seeking support from friends, family, and professional guidance cannot be overstated. Building a robust support network provides a lifeline during challenging times, offering understanding, empathy, and practical guidance.

Embracing personal growth and viewing challenges as opportunities for transformation become the cornerstones of resilience. Continuous growth involves self-reflection, a commitment to learning, and an intentional effort to adapt to evolving dynamics. Acknowledging and encouraging positive behavior becomes a catalyst for change. By reinforcing constructive actions, individuals contribute to the creation of an environment that nurtures growth and strengthens relationships.

As we look ahead, the transformative strategies presented in this journey serve as guiding principles for fostering harmony within the family unit. Striking a balance between empathy and setting boundaries is crucial. Empathy fosters understanding, while boundaries protect emotional well-being. A harmonious family dynamic involves a delicate interplay of both. Continued emphasis on effective communication ensures that family members stay connected. Navigating challenges with open dialogue and clear communication reinforces the unity of the family unit.

The importance of building and sustaining support networks remains a continuous endeavor. Friends, family, and professional guidance contribute to ongoing resilience and provide a safety net during challenging times. Integrating positive reinforcement into the family culture creates a foundation for constructive relationships. Celebrating positive moments, acknowledging efforts, and reinforcing shared values contribute to a positive and supportive atmosphere.

Recognizing that personal and familial growth is an ongoing process fosters a mindset of adaptability. Viewing challenges as opportunities and celebrating progress contribute to the collective evolution of the family. In moving forward, it's crucial to remember that transformation is not a destination but a continual journey. Each family member, including the mother-in-law, plays a role in this shared odyssey. By fostering a culture of empathy, effective communication, and continuous growth, families can navigate challenges with resilience and move forward with a shared commitment to harmony.

As we conclude this exploration, let these transformative principles be the compass guiding the path forward. May the journey be one of continual growth, understanding, and the enduring pursuit of familial harmony.

www.ingramcontent.com/pod-product-compliance
Lightning Source LLC
Chambersburg PA
CBHW060801260726
48660CB00002B/727